"The Eye that mocks a father,

that scorns obedience to a mother,

will be pecked out by the ravens in

the valley,

will be eaten by the vultures."

Proverbs 30.18 The Holy Bible

"A lesson that should be known to sons, daughters, and politicians,

I know because I was eaten by the vultures."

The author, Bryan Ray Cook

Chapter One

What Is, Reparations?

Reparations is money paid back to person or persons for mistakes or wrong done to

them by the offending person or persons. This is the simplest definition I can come up

with. This is what this book is about. My definition of reparations. I believe that my,

definition of reparations, is uniquely different from other people's definition and my publisher

is not paying me to use other people's definition to come up with my own

definition of reparations then, have it published. My publisher wants me to publish my own

concept of reparations that comes from my own heart and mental understanding of my own life

then publish it. Then maybe I will get paid for it to take care of my bills.

So, because like I am trying to pay my bills and fulfill my dreams from school, being I have debts to pay, so that is what I am doing.

So here it goes.

My concept of reparations back from my parents, who were at an age they could really

be called my grandparents.   Biologically speaking, they were my birth parents,

they had me late in life. As the old joke went if anyone knew me you would understand why

they had me so late in life. Ha, Ha, the readers got a good laugh for the day, so now continue

the story.

Originally as I understand it, America's current concept of reparations in American political

thought came from near the end of the Civil War when United States General Sherman

introduced, after consultation with African America pastors and activists in the South at the time came up with 40 acres and a mule. Sherman, the African American pastors, and

activists, conceived between them that is what it would take for a single African American

man, to provide food and self-reliance for himself. African American women, as I remember

from the time, were not granted 40 acres and a mule, only the African American men in the

area. If the ladies of the time wanted to be part of the action, they had to marry the men

to be involved. I believe that was how it was...I will have to look this up...let us hang on

to the thought and put it on hold, for now.

This was Union General Sherman's policy as his Union Troops occupied the Confederate

South. The policy would take effect in the coastal areas of Georgia and South Carolina until the end of the civil war. The white settlers and supporters of the Confederate South were kicked

out of the mansions by Sherman's Union troops, leaving the white occupants homeless.

However, finally the African American folk were paid back for the slavery they endured.

This concept is something that will be spoken about later in this book in a concept called

expropriation without compensation because this is a principle of that concept. A lot

of folks believe that to redress the income inequality and to balance out who wins

in our society and who has lost in this society historically and try to correct it, we should

take property from the rich and give to the poor to equal things out. The people whose

land was taken from them were people who took land or property from the present poor and dispossessed 'back in the day', so the government is just trying to correct

this injustice now. No compensation to the landowners, they can just "suck an egg" and

get over it.!!!!!!

Did the people who own and lives on this contested land have anything to do with the

the inequalities of the society present day. Some say they are benefitting from the injustices

of the past brought about by their ancestors. Is this true? Should a society pursue this course

of action?

It says in the bible, one should not judge. So, since I am a Christian, I am not. I know, what a

cop out.   I love to stay out of trouble, that is how I lived this long. Since I am neutral to this I

can see both sides of the issue. On the one hand, land and property, at some point in the future, should be returned to the rightful owners or people, peacefully without violence hopefully, but

returned. However, if several generations or centuries or more of time has passed. The

people living on the contested land who are generations of folk, descendants of folk who took

this contested land from the native inhabitants to begin with…should they be thrown off the land

and become the society's new homeless while the present native population take over the

former's holdings. Are not the people being forced to be homeless to correct past injustices?

Many generations and many, many years of time spanning centuries or more, now native people

to the society that they live, which has forced them into this homelessness to restore original

justice to the original inhabitants, isn't this wrong also?

Man, this is some deep stuff. And it is beginning to smell into high heaven too! Be prepared

to cover your nose.

I will be using other metaphors in this book, but this is a good start. Who settles conflicts,

like this. Usually government, through the court systems local state or federal, (United States).

If wrongs are being done to a certain group of citizens to benefit others, lawmakers or policy

makers such as city councilmen, mayors, state legislators, governors, federal legislators

(Senators and Congressmen) and Presidents (United States) make policy or laws, that by threat

of jail or prison to the offenders who offend that law, these laws work to equal things out. If

that does not work, people take to the streets and protest, (or cause public violence if desperate

enough, though it is not legal) to set things straight. This happened several times during the

12

existence of our country, with the Civil Rights movement being the most peaceful, with the

American Civil War being the most violent that I can think of. The example that I used,

Sherman's 40 acres and a mule, throwing out the white occupants and giving the plantations

to African Americans, is called Expropriation without compensation. Is this right. I do not

know. Maybe as I continue writing this book, we can figure this out.

How does our present-day government deal with the issue of reparations in this U.S?

After the Lincoln assassination, Andrew Johnson overturned Sherman's 40 acres and

a mule program, threw back out the African American people and put the white owners

of the plantation houses back in. What a flip flop…would not you think that is wrong.

Andrew Johnson also, paid back slave owners (yes you heard that right, slave owners)

for the slaves that were freed by the 13th, 14th, and 15th, amendments to the constitution.

(I believe that this only done with the former slave states loyal to the Union…but I

cannot remember for sure…I really had to dig just to find this much out!) This is

really a slap in the face in efforts to equalize things in our society and payback

African Americans for past slavery.

Here is another issue that might rattle our brains. There is talk that there should

equal rights for women. Women have endured unwanted sexual assaults since the

cave man days…should women as a group because of this be paid back reparations for

past sexual assaults that women in history were forced to endure and our enduring now,

14

especially in our country. Should women, as a group, be paid reparations ahead of African

Americans because criminal sexual assaults are more serious offenses than the slavery

endured by African Americans. Is criminal sexual assault more serious than the slavery

endured by African Americans, ergo women as a group in society (and I am including

African American women in this group) more deserving of reparations than African

Americans.

Man, have I raised a lot of questions and stirred the pot up something fierce,

It is really beginning to smell now! Let us give ourselves a good GI shower, get really

clean, put on our HAZ-MAT suits, and see what we together can come up with to solve the Reparations problem in the United States?

What are some of the challenges, world governments have tried to handle reparations problems of its citizens?

Chapter Two

What Form Should Reparations Take?

Now that we are properly scrubbed, wearing our hazmat suits, and protected ourselves from

stench of our country's unresolved reparations issues: here are some ways that we can pay back

our short-changed brothers and sisters for the wrongs in the past and present day according to what I have seen or read in the news:

Payout: One-time payout to our society's shortchanged to even things out and we can say we did something to address the past and sins of the present.

Pension: Give the shortchanged people and the disposed a pension, so much per month until they die, as income assistance to solve the reparations issue.

Bonds: Sell bonds to public to either provide pension or payout options to the shortchanged and dispossessed of our society, (U.S. Treasury Bonds.)

Baby: Federal Government set aside 'Baby Bonds' invested by U.S. citizens through treasury to provide low income children identified by Federal Government a certain amount of money they would have access to when they turn 21.

Land: Government gives land to dispossessed and shortchanged of our population.

Courts: Courts forces individuals and companies to pay restitution to dispossessed and short-changed members of our population to reduce income and other types of inequality.

Individual: Individuals on their own try to solve reparations problems.

Bank: African Americans or shortchanged, disposed populations form their own financial system separate from society's recognized financial system to address their concerns.

Church: James Forman interrupted service in 1960's demanding church pay reparations to African Americans for past slavery.

Stock: Some ideas have been kicked around that U.S. government purchases private stock to give to dispossessed and shortchanged members of our society, or at least U.S. government breaks wall street up enough to give the dispossessed and shortchanged members of our society more access to private stock to better increase the dispossessed and shortchanged members of our population financially bolstering shoring up and strengthening our economy.

Tax Break: Government gives tax break for individuals and private businesses to contribute to government fund for reparations. (To African Americans).

Gender Tax: Tax men and give excess to women to balance everyone's yearly income out.

The next 12 chapters focuses on these proposed solutions. Of all the proposals I have mentioned, the Tax Break option is a government-private enterprise, while the Individual and Church proposals are private and public. The remaining reparation ideas are government.

Chapter Three

Payout?

Say one is a single dude, (or woman). You could be single person with kids and

old folks to care for. You are going to need to get your refund…and whatever money

you need to get. Then one shining day, the U.S. government gives the neighbors next

door several million dollars because in their past, their ancestors were slaves. They

who was once in a jam as you are in now, are living very well as millionaires, Go Figure!

Though as you deal with your old folks, kids, all by yourself, single at that and hoping

to take care of your responsibilities without making your boss mad and losing your job,

the job you need to make all your ends meet in taking care of them, then finding out

your neighbors get free money from the U.S. government over a historical issue now

living the 'high' life. You are not feeling good right now to say the least!
(Do not go

serial against your neighbors, that is illegal!) How would you feel?

I tried to leave race out of the equation because using black and white
in the

example above would be perceived as racist though African Americans
were, of

course, once slaves in the U.S.

"WHO IS THE TURKEY?"

"Your Side-Show!"

Let say you, the single person (either gender) are caring for kids

that are not yours and old folks who have dementia are yours, you are
white. Because of some

'side show' that went down with relatives who never talked to you in this
life, you are caring

for those anal relative's kids because you want to make sure they are not
in the Foster Care

22

system being 'shucked around' not knowing who their mom or dad were and no good

role model, possibly being homeless or killed. You 'person up' and become the role model

showing the children, you are a good role model by giving them a home.

   You are caring for your old folks, so they do not go to the old-folks home and possibly

become homeless or die on the street. So now you are caring for the kids who are not yours and

your old folks on a very skimpy retail pay you earn, taking care of customers at some retail store

you do not own…just like the kids, you and your senile mom and dad, live in a

home you do not own. You are working long hours now

never home hoping the kids and your senile old folks do not accidentally blow up the neighborhood by leaving the gas on the stove on or something, so you, those kids, and

your senile old folks can live in a reasonable home hoping it do not get run down…though

you do not own it, driving a car you do not own so you can get around hoping to keep it

and the house you live in paid for on skimpy weekly retail check. Man, now you can

really show the neighbors now how 'woke' you really are! How you are keeping your

'side-show' together, your new immediate family together! You are better than your

neighbors next door who do not work at a real job, who they and their kids are

alcoholics and drug addicts. You hope these neighbors are not drug dealers

because you live next door and you do not want to be swept up in some FBI/DEA drug raid. You know that they are this way because these white neighbors are seriously

depressed about being of Armenian descent.

"The Armenian Genocide"

I am relying on my memory from World History in college I took at East Texas State University

in getting my bachelor's in political science in the early 1980's at least 30 plus years ago, (I am

fifty-four now.) so bear with me. In the early 1900's (1900-1918), the Muslim Turks went

against Armenian folk who were mostly settled in eastern Antonia because the Christian

Armenians were economically better off than the Turkish Muslims in the declining

Ottoman Empire. Young Muslims Turks took over the government of the declining

Ottoman Empire before World War I, (by force I think, this was an empire not a democracy)

25

and began measures to marginalize and finally exterminate the Armenian people (some

historians contest this was a systematic extermination of the Armenians, different from the

no dispute of Germans exterminating the Jewish people in World War II). Estimates

of the executions of Armenians, I think one and a half million as I recall, occurred between

the dates, I hazily remember from my college course in World History thirty plus years ago, of

1912 through 1922. In World War I, the declining Ottoman Empire sided with Germany.

At the time of the end of World War I, Germany was defeated, and the Ottoman empire ended,

(I hope I am right on this concerning the end of the Ottoman empire). Over time the successor

state, The Republic of Turkey, came to be and the Armenian executions ended I believe before

1925. The number rolling around my head from the World History class I took thirty plus years

ago, of one and a half million executed Armenians keeps rolling around in my head. To this day I

believe the descendants of Armenians were never repaid for this, as with descendants of African

American slaves were never paid back for their enslavement here in the U.S. despite many

government apologies.

Talk is cheap.

Now Back To, Your Sideshow:

You are working hard at a low paying retail job to keep your family together (your old

folks and the children you are caring for who are not yours but your kin because they are

in prison for doing something stupid) and all the neighbors, newspapers, community leaders praise what a 'good soul' you are for caring for your family the way you do on a shoestring

and in debt. (Though no one knows this and you because of the good up-bringing and manners

your moral parents raised you with you do not say anything, but like that was stated, talk is cheap

and you do wish the community, or the town would give you a little bit of money to 'help you

out'.

   Suddenly, there is one of many Arab Springs going on with our native ally Turkey.

For leaving the Kurds high and dry as they fought with us the United States to take down

ISIS (Another story that one can read about on their own.) and fighting them out of their own homeland,

 Kurdistan which is Turkey's 'security zone', to appease the United States

and Western powers, they pay back all Armenians living everywhere for the genocide they

28

suffered and the destruction of their nation and people. Your neighbors, (U.S. Armenians)

get a check of several million dollars from Turkey and the community, press, and politicians

praise the blessings these people receive while you are no longer in the spotlight for all your

good deeds you are financing on your debt in your name. Suddenly you are this single

person, man or woman, more than likely a woman, taking care of all your problems alone. Who

is the 'Turkey' now. You!!!!!

I lay this example out because bad things happen to people, whoever you are, by the stupidity

or arrogance of others. People who say, 'well it's the Lord's doing' if they believe in God at all,

is not true. God is independent from this because he gave mankind free-will. So, the blame should go to the arrogant, hence reparations to the marginalized (shafted). Race, gender, or

any other distinctive factor of people has nothing to do with it. It is the cruelty of the human

heart that has everything to do with it. People who are victims for whatever reason have the

right to be paid back for the sins of the past, which is why we have the mechanism of law and

government to do this. This example I pointed out was purposely using white folk in

these circumstances because if the world of humanity was totally white, all white folks

would fight and oppress each other for other reasons. Race or gender, therefore, is not a factor,

it is just another reason for people to be bullies when they **should not be!**

Should Payout be the way to settle reparations issues. As I tried to point out in my,

'Turkey' example, some government paying out reparations to private citizens could really anger among neighbors and would be bad government planning. In our country

I know that there is bad anger, bad injustice against people. Should the LGBTQ people

be marginalized (single out for ridicule) or be victims of violence. Of course not, it is

their life, what those people do is none of my business. I am a nice guy. I believe in the

 Holy Father, Son, and Holy Ghost's call He will have to make with his children. I

am just trying to get along with his children on the good side…that is all I can do…and with

my fellow Americans, who more than likely have been shafted by others before they met me,

that is the best that I can accomplish with the people of my country, Americans do not trust

each other because we hurt each other so much…why should we collectively trust other countries who do the same or worse with their own people.

My publisher wanted to express my view of things before anything I write and that is

what should be allowed into the library network the publisher has with people in this

country because it is real and not fake. This is what people really want. I need to be real.

To the people who I thank for reading this book I, like anyone else, maybe be from

Texas, but I am neither Jesus Christ nor David Koresh. I have told white lies at work

when my boss by mistake complimented me for work others did, I had viscous verbal

arguments with my parents (who have now passed) on how things should be, or what

they should do with me, or what they can do for me (do not worry, nothing physical, like

I am telling you readers I am not David Koresh! Or the Incredible Hulk.) the arguments

32

were non-threatening. Just spirited and loudly verbal, like most families.
I got mad a lot

of the times at a lot of people when I should not. I also got hot headed in
arguments with

chicks to whom I wanted to take out who would not go out with me,
which I know was wrong,

undignified, and off. I have made mistakes, nothing criminal, but as
others who exist in

a normal sane life do as I do, I, like others, have made mistakes and said
things I now regret.

   Sometimes people's regrets can lead a man or a woman to go into
'freak out mode'. It

does happen and it is horrible but if I may say by taking a guess, this is a
rare event though

it is magnified by our social media, TV, newspapers, and radio. Most
people just want to be

accepted by their fellows as I do. Most of the time that is hell whether it
is in job, family friends,

33

or love. Each of us, man or woman, is surrounded by people and we want to notice us as well

as the community that they hope will notice them whether it is local, state, or national. Because

we live in a fluid democracy, in a fluid republic, every man or woman in this country is torn by

political divides whether it is in the family or outside the family. I cannot even use the word

family because the siblings that I have spoken with out and about in the community all the

time are children of divorce. Most of the time, boy or girl who are now man and woman, do

not have a sense of identity because their family had dissolved itself by divorce. They as

potential parents in our republic do not even know if they should form families because of

the dissolution of their parents from the committed marriage that begat them, man or woman.

One result of this is a serious drop in the replacement rate of people dying off by the creation

of the newborn of that society. This is not a research book. I have written one, but that is not

this. I am just calling things as I see them or process them in my mind for this is the only

literature my publisher's library network will accept so they will not be sued by other authors.

This is a good thing because I have to say things here that come from my own heart and

mind. I hope what I share here of my problems here and in other chapters, as well as

my own take that I processed firsthand from media or word of mouth. I am not a lawyer

though I wanted to be one, but I never got the money (another teaser for later in this

book) but I will try to summarize my rambling in the chapter. The payout by government option, in my opinion, would not work because you would cause more dissension among the

population as the government 'plays God'... deciding who should be rich and who should be

poor as individuals from all races and backgrounds struggle to make ends meet for them or

theirs, as in my Turkey example. This act could cause more, and I am speaking here I hope

metaphorically, people to go over the edge and possibly become the next active psycho, but

more than likely be more alcoholics or drug-attics, which society does not need, let alone the

individuals affected, need. One-time payout may momentarily help the disadvantaged and the

economy momentarily...but soon will be whisked away after the beneficiaries buy their dope

or boos. Society again later stuck with the same problems again, and after the euphoria of the payout goes away, what do we do now to end society's ills more permanently. (Teaser:

the Turkey skit is done for now…but there is a reason for it, and you will see mention of

Turkey, the country, in later chapters for a reason.

Chapter Four

Pension?

"Fantasy Island"

Free Pension! Yeah lay it on me, I can be anything I want to be. Man, I can be

the tooth-ferry! Hey man I wanted to be the Tinman from the Wizard of Oz.

Maybe I can be Dorothy!!! Wow what a paradise. Hey if they legalize drugs

maybe I can do some heroin, some marijuana, I do not care what it is, if

I can smoke that peace pipe! Hey, man I do not care about showing up for

anything important. I do not want to be responsible and have a family! I do not

want to be responsible for anything!

Responsible! I do not want to be responsible! I want to have fun. If life is not pleasurable it is not worth living. I want to do whatever I want whenever I want! You, you, you,

are not my Daddy! Shut your mouth! Get out my face!

 What I have described is a society that operates on the concept of Secular Humanism as

(in my opinion) is preached and practiced by the cultural elite in Hollywood and a lot of our,

political elite in Washington. The United States, the world between 1960 and 1970 were going

to go this direction because of the wars, economic turmoil, questioning of the roles

of genders in our society or other nations. Democratic socialism is the mechanism

of which this would be brought about, everyone gets a pension, no one is responsible,

just have fun. This cannot be done because society would break down if society's people

are not responsible…so the example I just stated is just 'Fantasy Island'.

Keep this thought in mind as I describe the difference between a Pension and a Payout. A

Payout is a 'one-time Johnny' payment to make a restitution for a wrong. Divorce in the United

States between equal partners-has one partner paying off the other partner to get rid

of them and move on to 'greener pastures', a payout is what companies pay

managers or employees to get rid of them (severance), and governments

uses to settle claims with groups of citizens who were mistreated by that government

(reparations, such as U.S. government paying Japanese citizens who were detained

by U.S. government in WWII.). To sum up Payout is a one-time payment to make

amends with another party and move on to something or someone else.

Pension is a different concept. In the old days, pension is what was paid to

soldiers, first responders, people who worked for government, after many years

of service to that government, (local, state, federal). Companies also paid pensions

to their employees after many years of service to that company. This is not done

mostly in the private sector now, you are giving a savings account of money to,

if you were wise, keep in your savings and let it grow and is meant to be a supplement savings

to social security, any military pay, or healthcare benefit by the government or governments,

local, state, or federal (this is my understanding of my 401k plan I will consult with my HR

person to see if I have this in my mind correctly). A pension is an allotment of cash paid per month by a government or a business for the longtime service and commitment of a

person to that business or government entity for the life of the person. The definition

of a pension has in its definition and in its being the fact that one (man or woman) had

to serve an entity by their work and in return from that entity they would receive a

weekly or biweekly (in some cases by the month) paycheck and when you get a

certain age as after you gave faithful committed service to that government or private

entity, a pension. So, the people of Woodstock believe that all their pleasures will

be fulfilled without work have probably realized by now that cannot happen because from

all people's work comes the financing essential for private companies and governments at all levels of American society whether it is a business getting their revenue from goods or

services sold produced from people paid for their work, or our government entities getting it is

tax from goods or services sold from people paid for their work to produce those goods and

services   The National or Federal Government is different because the Federal government

has the power of the mint to produce money. However, our Federal Government does not

live within its means because right now it is in debt to U.S. treasury bond holders 22 trillion

plus, dollars. State Governments, County Governments, local governments, individuals,

businesses, and school districts do not have the luxury of the having a mint or a printing

press to print legal money, so all those entities must live within a balanced or budget (or should live within a balanced budget though many of the entities I just mentioned

are 'under water' financially, owing more than what is coming in to pay the bills) to

serve their people or themselves as individuals. I am grateful in living in a land where

I can express myself anyway I want and criticize my government when I feel it is needed

without retribution. However, I cannot shout 'Fire' in a crowded theatre, scaring the people

in the theatre into a frenzy, I should and would be arrested for doing something that stupid.

My summation from all this is that you have the right of freedom of expression, but you must

be responsible. Sex is a medium and if done wrong someone can be seriously damaged

psychologically. Freedom of speech is fine, but you must be responsible, or you could cause public chaos.   People do not get a pension who do not work. My final point of

all this is you must have done something in life worthwhile contributing to your community

to earn your pension from whatever entity that hired you whether it is a private firm or

government entity, money does not just come out of the sky, so freedom is not free.

Here is another message, there is no such thing as free love. Love for one thing is

not sex, and sex is not love. These words are not interchangeable terms. Love is not sex, sex

is not love. Love (Romantic) is the caring of another being, human of course, above all

else, Sex is a medium of expression of which it is carried out. When we love, God meant for us

use the medium of sex responsibility, it was not meant to be a recreational activity

of which it is something to use to feel good, not actually to love one or other

as people. In this debacle…sex is being used to fulfill the need of lust, a selfish

desire. The government will only pay you a pension if you served in a war or got disabled

(or are disabled from other causes). The government (U.S. government) is not going to pay

you a pension so you can have a good time. Get a job!

Now should African American descendants get a pension for their ancestors. That is

something that can be talked about. Yes, the white man enslaved those people, in some

cases completed minor cases of genocide against them because they were thought of nothing

more as livestock of which the population should be balanced. The U.S. Constitution at

one time only thought of African Americans as three fifths of a person, the white slaveholding families thought less of them than that. A reason why Thomas Jefferson preached for freedom

for all on the one hand and raped his African American female slave on the other. Humans are

are good at saying one thing and doing another and we are all guilty of it including me…that is

why I am saying all the time I am no Jesus…and I am no David Koresh either (I am a Texas

homeboy) unlike Thomas Jefferson I am not into rape, and if he was such a great guy

proclaiming freedom for all including slaves…what made him flip to do that! That is a

question that I wish history would answer for me.

   After the Civil War, Callie House (my high school history of names bites so I do not know

if I remember this right but I think I am close, this book is not a research book or paper but my own take own what should be done about unequal income inequality for our country, so

forgive me.) and others was trying to form a movement to create a pension for slaves, (like

social security…S.S. I….veteran's benefits, disability benefits of today.) This effort

went from 1865 through around 1912 when a New York Times article stated that Callie

House and folk were busted for mail fraud as Callie tried to solicit money by mail to

get the U.S. government to pay an ex-slave pension to ex-slaves. Was this true or

was this a get-even from the white establishment, I have no idea, I am just recanting

all this from high school and beginning college memory. On Juneteenth 2019 there

was finally an airing out of John Conyers bill, H.R. 40, in front of a U.S. House committee to commission a study asking if the Federal Government should pay out

reparations to African Americans and how. This bill never was mentioned again

…all anyone heard was how to impeach Trump. Will this get out of committee?

That my friend is unknown?

   There is an Equal Rights Amendment, way back in my mother's time. Creating equal

pay between men and women and equal civil rights between men and women which includes

a woman having complete control over her being including reproduction (abortion, antiabortion

stuff). My mother was into all that because the boss did not pay her equal to the guys doing

the same job. Now it is ratified but it is several years late and several dollars short, (the

amendment had a deadline to get ratified by most states after the Congress of

50

the 1970's in both houses passed it.). Should we forego that deadline and let it take effect now?

Should pensions be a way to deal with reparations or payout be the way? Should Reparations

happen at all? I do not know but I will give my advice on what I think should be done in the

later chapters of this books.

Chapter Five

Bonds?

Bonds, this is a word that describes a lot of things. First, I want to talk about family

bonds. I drank a lot because there were pressures in my family household. We were

not a nuclear family (no not the bomb). I was the only child in the Cook household.

We all got along well!   We though, had very spirited agreements, and we had some

very spirited arguments. When it came to family finances, we were like the Prince

song "When Doves Cry". We were a lower middle-class white family that argued

over money. My family was Democrats, When, it came to who wore the pants in

the family let us face it; it was my mother. She made sure that our money was not

spent on foolish things…when my father did override her and did what he felt he could had to do for the family anyway…man did he hear about it. The line in the song

"…she was never satisfied" that was my mom. Do not get me wrong, she was

a good mother. She had her ways though. No one ever touched the money without

her consent, when my father overrode my mother on the money issue, he faced her

wrath…and I overheard that wrath. Nights when I went to bed when I was young

I heard them argue bitterly over money. I got along with my parents though I too faced bitter

verbal wrath over both when I did not please them.

   Most of these disagreements were minor, not coming home on time, waking up and

interfering with her important discussions with other female neighbors In Dallas it

was with other mothers about my schooling, as she and I got older it was with other female nurses about my father's elder care until he passed, I think 2012. In either case

when I came in after waking up from bed to go to work at my retail job, she would

tell me to "Go to my Room!" like "Jamie Go To, Your Room" from 'Happy Days'

so, my mother can discuss her business with whoever was there. Sometimes, my first

cousin females and a husband to one of my first cousins would come over to 'shoot the

breeze' with my mother, or mother and father when he was alive, the husband to one

of one of my first cousins would say "What is That?" when my mother told me go

to my room as if I were a little kid…and I was at the time at my various ages of 40+.

Some of these disagreements were 'pretty bad'. In most households when the man and woman are grown, in Texas it is 18, if it is consensual, they marry and start their own home.

Why did I live with my parents for so exceptionally long, am I a bum? No, I worked in retail all my life

since I was 18 in retail to help support my elder kin, my parents when they were alive, and

first cousin and her husband now. I do this now by paying the rent and helping with paying the

maintenance expenses. My thinking is why pay a faceless corporation or strangers rent and

maintenance expenses when I can pay my family members the rent and maintenance expenses to

help them out financially. When it came to finding a lady mate in my life the fish were not

biting…so what I described above is what I did.

So, when I stayed with my parents, I said I would care for them until God took them home,

(passed or died and went to God). I asked though that I would receive the property if I cared them until then. They said yes. So, I took them to all the doctors and all the places necessary

to keep them going (the VA, eye doctors, supplementary doctors, one thing that happens

when you get old…you need to see doctors…so I took them there.) In return I asked my,

Dad and Mom for the five acres for my future use because I may sell it later for money

to get married and raise a family on. As I cared for mother and father, I worked, (and

still work) for a retail chain. I was tired and almost ready to pass out one night when

I came home. The following morning, I told my parents I hope that one day a rich

beautiful woman would 'parachute in', marry me, take care of me, and my financial

problems. I of course was telling a joke and again I was feeling really fatigued and tired from everything hard that I done before, (at the time I worked in the lawn and

garden department of the chain I worked for). My elderly parents told me if I ever got married

I would never get the house. I got mad, yelled at the decibels of a nuclear bomb going off,

and ran out the door. I drank some heavy spirits, drove home drunk. My mom was hacked

that I was drunk and that created a wedge between us, an eternal one. Later, after my father

passed, it was just my mother and me. She forgave me for that incident, and we had a 'Affidavit

of Heirship' done so it would be clear the property would be left to me. I waited until the last

minute to put her in a home because she was giving me hell for even thinking about it. But I

finally got her in a home., I did what was necessary to keep her alive, my mother respected that and loved me for it...but the State (Texas) was still giving hell to get her property instead

of me inheriting it. To settle this once and for all, my attorney drew up a "Lady Bird Deed" and

I was getting my mother to sign it, she did not, I had one of my cousins try to get her to sign it,

Mother did not. So, I lost the property to the State of Texas. I of course was hurt...but I kept

that pain out of site, so my mother knew that I loved her during the final time she had before

my mother passed. Though as she was passing from this Earth to be with God, she knew I

loved her and I knew she loved me. That night however when I got mad and drank out of the

house, and the property issue itself created an eternal wedge, even to this day after my mother's

passing, between mother and I that only the holy God can intervene and forgive. In all the time

I came to be on this Earth, I never knew where I was with my mother, and because of that I

knew where I was with my fellow American citizens. That insecurity was probably the reason

why my view of things never came to be, I will expand on this later in this book and how

it relates to my view on reparations.

As to the issue of using bonds to deal with reparations issue in this country. When I was in

my seventh and eighth grade government I learned that taxpayers did not want to pay reparations

to descendants of African Americans present day because it would increase taxes. My seventh or

eighth grade government student answer to that was to sell a U.S. Treasury bond specifically

earmarked for that purpose and leave the taxes alone. The interest earned from that U.S.

government bond would attract families and individual to invest in government reparations

60

bond, interest paid to them from government would be the attraction, since the government

owned the U.S. mint, unlike the other levels of government in our country (State, local, school,

and so on) they can print just enough money to put into circulation to cover it, and not raise taxes

to U.S. taxpayers.

"God I'm Socrates!" I exclaimed in class. The teacher, who was a football coach teaching this

just to satisfy the principle so he can do what he wanted, coach football. I thought I was

bitching and everyone would notice me. They did not...they loved the football coach.

He was the worrier he and his J.R. High football team were winning games every Friday

night. I was just the nerd. "Bryan! did you ever fail to consider the country's economic cycle?

If our economy is in recession there is less money produced to tax…therefore

the government would have to raise money on taxpayers to honor your stupid government

bond. So there!!! Any more attitude like that and you will be expelled!".

"Yes sir!", I said.

Well did I have the air let out my balloon. So much for school memories!

Later, Max Kiesure, in 2008, came up with same idea, his Black Liberation Bonds 'bombed'.

Whether I was in school or college, I learned that James Foreman and the Black Economic

Development Council interrupted a white Jewish service to demand their church or churches

(white Jewish churches and white people as a whole) to pay back African Americans for

slavery. $50,000,000,000 I think (if it is more than the $1,000 in my savings account, at any given time, people are breathing higher oxygen content than me, if I tried to breath

this $50B oxygen content these people are breathing or trying to breathe, I would be brain dead

from the blast, I like most people, am not used to that much oxygen.) That is when I started

to try to figure out a private option for reparations that did not involve the government I will

mention the later at the end of my book. The fallacy of using a government bond to pay back

historical wrongs done to people is blatantly clear. It is great when the U.S. Economy is great to

use this approach, but when the economy goes down, people cannot find jobs, and the taxes go

up by the government to pay its obligations, then this is not a good option…another

option needs to be considered to right historical wrongs done to people that does not burden modern day taxpayers unnecessarily.

Bonds are issued by Corporations, Governments, and other concerns to raise money

to pay for projects to either make profit or benefit a community. The people in the community

trust that these people will pay back the bond with interest, and the people use the interest of

bond to pay for their children's college or save for future use by their children. Trust between

people are essential for the financial instrument of the bond to work.

I killed the bond between my mother and I over the conflict of the property I had hope

to inherit from my mother when I put her in a home as I was pushed by Texas Adult Protective

Services to do so. They threatened to put me in jail if I did not do as they said.

I did not kill the love between my mother and I, if one is a civilized being, nothing should kill the love between mother and son. The trust between mother and son, a

product of which is a bond between you and her, I killed, because I was forced by Adult

Protective services in Texas to put her in a home because it was law…she could not think

for herself anymore. My mother did not want to be put in some room somewhere against

her will, her money taken away from her because her mind was going…in a way I cannot

blame her…she did not commit a crime, who would want that. Because of Adult Protective

Services of Texas, however, I and my relatives had to put her in a Senior Citizen Home and

use her savings for her care. My state forced me to do something I did not want to do, betray

my mother and her wishes. She was in a home…she was treated well with all the modern technology that was available…but she passed peacefully. My inheritance in the Affidavit

of Heirship I was had with her had turned to dust, the document was as worthless as toilet

paper. In fact, I should give it to someone who needs it for toilet paper. Two years after she

passed, Texas finally woke up and the State (Texas) had finally put in writing that they were

taking the property, what can I say…give to Cesar and to God what is God's…that is the law.

I am sorry that I and my relatives had to put my elderly mom in the old folks, home against

her wishes…she loved her freedom and the fact she had money of her own in this life…

something that had not happen for a lot of women until the advent of modern times…for

the United States…at least until after the Civil War. My mother was mad she lost her money…but most of all, her freedom…and she has not ever committed any type of crime

or anything…but still lost her freedom. I did not want to put her in a home, but I was

forced to by my state…my inheritance to be sold now going to pay her bills under the U.S.

Medicaid Recovery Program.

Is the right, is this wrong, I do not know, it just is. I will go into more struggles about

this that is going on with me and how this relates to my reparation ideas in the Land

chapter of this book. I know this if a government loses its bond with its people, its money,

stocks, other securities such as checks and financial instruments, **_and private or public bonds,_**

their value will spiral downward, the economy will go into freefall. Society will collapse. Then

you have complete anarchy…dog eat dog!

Chapter Six: Baby?

"Don't be such a baby!", my mother would exclaim, my father would exclaim, and now

my boss exclaims when he gripes me out because I have not done something right. I was

putting up a basket of shop backs (returned or abandoned merchandise). I did not ask

anyone's permission, I just did it. They were hardware shop backs, I work for a retail

store and chain that sold anything that anyone needed. I worked in toys but the boss

could not get anyone else to come in to work their departments, so the faithful, I am being

one, picked up the slack. I cried and cried and bitched, oh woe is me!!!!!!!!!!!!!!!!1

Oh, Woe is Me!!!!!!!!!!!Why do I have to this, oh woe is me!!!!!!!!!!!!.... This is not

my department, why are you dumping this on me!!!!My Boss said "I know that this is not your job, but aren't you glad you have a job????So be quiet and clean everything

up.!!!!" I would say afterward, "Yes sir!!!!!"

Yeah, I am a cry baby, that is probably why I am still single. I am fifty-four or fifty-five

and still need to grow up.

My Ma and Dad thought I was a cry baby…probably why I had problems with my inheritance.

I was always a doormat. Ladies (non-married) probably thought I was a

"cry baby" which is why I was invisible to them. Guys thought I was a "cry baby", which

why I was pushed aside when they promoted themselves to the public eye or to economic

opportunities. Will I come up with something that will get me the respect of my peers.

Only the God of my understanding, my higher power, can tell me. We will see.

Somewhere, I remember a Professor named William Darity (I hope I have his

last name spelled right) came up with "Baby Bonds" program which U.S. Treasury

bonds would be sold to establish $20,000 for children of poor families (all races,

backgrounds, religions, and I also think LGBTQ), only qualification is that they are

below the poverty level yearly income of families in these United States so when

these poor children grew up, they would have this $20,000 kickoff in the bank to

give their adulthood a kickstart. Nice program but as with the "Black Liberation

Bonds" idea in chapters back, (bonds), if there is a downturn in the economy

no one wants to pay for everyone else's children to succeed when they and the taxpayers' children have, to do without to pay more in taxes so our U.S. government entities

can fulfills their obligations to their pay for the 'baby bonds.' This will not pass in Congress,

(or anywhere else at any level of government in the United States) This was the State of Texas's

government's attitude as it seized my inheritance in restitution for the taxpayers for caring for

my mother in a State-run nursing home as specialists were paid by the taxpayers to extend

my mother's life as-long-as possible, until she passed. When sold, my inheritance being seized by

the state, would be sold and the money would be put in the General Revenue fund of the State

of Texas so the state will pay back the Medicaid Recovery Program. Texas

taxpayers do not want to pay for the extended health care of my mother. So, Texas does this.

Some other reparations program will have to be thought up to deal with our reparations

problem.

Wow! This was a 'baby' of a chapter. Some chapters I write will be long and some short.

I hope I did not 'through the baby out with the bath water' here as we move on to the next

chapter of my book.

Chapter Seven: Land?

I talked about how I lost my inheritance because my Ma did not want to be in

Senior Citizen home as well as I should have taken care of her and not give in to Adult

Protective Services order to put her in the home. The State of Texas as we speak is seizing

property per contract I signed to put her in the home against her will which I clearly let

Adult Protective Services know was against her will, I did not want to go against her will

but Adult Protective Services forced me to do as if they were mobsters anyway and made

me do it. I lost the property because mother would not, afterward, sign the 'Lady Bird Deed'

a Texas legal instrument that would have kept the property in my hands because I was forced

to put her there. So, I lost my inheritance, I lost my family's land I was supposed to inherit…

I was not happy…but what could I do…" Give to Cesar what is Cesar's
What

is God's that is God's." Do I blame the State for this situation, or do I
blame mother? It is

what I said before…do not let the inheritance issue destroy the bond
between you and your

(in my case) Mother…even if you are homeless for a time…you want
your mother to pass

to the Lord in peace as she knows you love her…Though she knew I
loved her, I let this

inheritance issue be a wedge between us…leaving a big 'black hole'
between mother and I as she

passed…a 'black hole' of sadness that I would not wish for anyone else
for which is the reason

I mention this. A 'black hole' of sadness that I carry to this day….

Toward the end of the U.S. Civil War, General Sherman of the United
States Union

forces issued a special order to 15 to give each African American (men I
believe at the

time were the only ones that this was applied to…if women wanted to improve her

station in life there, she had to marry the black man, I am not sure about this part so

do not hold me to this) '40 acres and a mule' to an African American male or family

for free a payback for the enslavement of their ancestors before them. Mansions were

'using the lingo of our day 'flipped'' or sold to finance this program. Mansions were

seized from plantation owners to be sold for this to make a correction for the past

crimes of slavery or given to African American families to own for free for restitution.

Is this the right thing to do. I say the white plantation owners committed a clear crime

so, my heart would not break over it…give their possessions to African Americans for restitution for past slavery crimes, more power to them.

Here recently I watched a Fox tv show Tucker Carlson tonight where South Africa is trying

to in their constitution that the dark-skinned leaders of the government is putting a new

amendment into the post-Apartheid government of South African government that gave

dark skinned leader's power, that would allow the government to seize land without

compensation to be distributed to less fortunate dark-skinned farmers or dark skinned

people that would like to be farmers. Though Nelson Mandela busted up Apartheid

(from the concentration of political power to white people power of government to the

diversity of all the peoples as equals which gave majority of power to dark skinned people

of South Africa (people of color). Though the diversity of political power was achieved, a few white families own over 90% of the land…which is now the present point of

contention between the dark-skinned government and the few wealthy white families who

own most of the property of South Africa. Nelson Mandela saw this coming, so he

had a buyback program in which the new dark-skinned leadership would buy back

property from the white government, after the property was bought back, the property would

then be redistributed to the dark-skinned famers, would be farmers, and people for their use.

The new post Mandela leadership however believe that this land reform program is too

slow…more extreme measures need to happen. This new leadership of people of color

wants to take the property of the white families without buyback…some extreme elements want to take the white family owned property right now with no compensation...others

want to do it more slowly...starting with abandoned private and government property first

then work their way to the white family land. One way or the other...they plan to pass a

South African constitution amendment to do this and go after the white owned land and

redistribute the property to the rest of the population more evenly, empowering all the

people with capital for production and self-determination. Is this cool. For one thing

South Africa is not my country, so this is just an intellectual curiosity of study for me.

On the one hand as I mentioned and probably will mention again later in this book, I signed

a contract with the State of Texas saying they can take my personal assets (land) to pay for my mother's health, which is what I have done. Because I stayed with my mother for

a long time I found an attorney and established guardianship as well as try to qualify for

an exemption allowed under Texas law to try to avoid losing my inheritance and giving

my property to the State of Texas to pay my health care costs to keep her alive if

possible. The property is valued at between $35 to $60k. It hurt when they took it, but

I had to move on to other things in my life, such as developing an investment model for

reparations palatable to everyone that I will later discuss in this book. On the other

hand it would not bother me that the people of color leadership is South Africa seize

the white families land in South Africa and redistribute it, just as it did not bother me that Sherman seized the mansions and property and gave ownership to its former

slaves, the African Americans. If it stayed that way…we would not have the racial

and gender problems we have now.   However, I feel the white families' owner's pain

of have their land, worth millions, maybe billions seized and redistributed. This current

generation of white folk did not have anything to do with Apartheid or the slavery of

people of color by South Africa's white ancestors in the past, why should they pay for

the sins of their ancestors?   Is there some compromise? Keep reading.

Chapter Eight: Courts?

What is my experience in a court room? I went to Traffic court (which is a city level court)

to get some traffic tickets paid or expunged. On a 'hot day' in Rockwall County some

years back I walked into the county courthouse to get a drink…I took a shortcut through

a courtroom I thought was empty…it was not. I wound up stepping into a murder trial.

"Oops!!!I am sorry!" I told the Bailiff, he smiled and said "Don't worry about it, Coke

machine has been moved…it is down around the corner!", I said "Thank You Sir, have

a good one." and I of course left and found the machine.

I watch Judge Judy which depresses my faith in humanity including myself.

I quit watching it.

The following happened after my inheritance of land was seized by Texas government.

I had a nervous breakdown last year, a girl I liked did not like me, my landlord's dog

bit me...my boss did bite me (L.O.L!!!!), but I still have my job. I went to work

one day drunk...my boss laughed and told me to go to rehab if, I want to keep my job.

I went to rehab and learned how alcohol can be addictive and destroy brain cells. Saw

even on an X-ray...so I quit and was told my brain would heal completely in 24 months, I

went back to work and never drank again. I have had the honor of chairing of some of the

12 step meetings that dealt with people to prevent them from dinking again. I had to sign

papers acknowledging to their probation officers they were there. I was lucky I was caught

by my boss and not police or State Trooper...I could be arrested for DWI and served some serious time like the people whose papers I was signing for their probation officer as they

just came out of prison into the world after serving serious time in State prison. After realizing

this I am glad that I stopped doing the stupid stuff that could have me sent to State Prison or

got somebody killed I did not mean too, because of my stupid habit of drinking alcohol. I am

four months sober at the time of this writing. I intend to stay this way.

During the 1990's and 2000's, African Americans tried to sue Corporations who aligned

themselves with slavery during late 1800's and U.S. Civil War and used the slaves to operate

their businesses. None of the suits I know of won, except in California where I believe some

had to pay restitution to descendants of African American slaves. Is this a way to gain restitution

African American slaves or anyone else. Nice idea, but it only worked in California some isolated parts in the country…but not a nation as whole because institutionally

though our government apologized, the U.S. is not ready to pay out reparations to African

Americans yet.

Well wait a minute Bro, did not the Japanese Americans get reparations for

detained in WWII. Have not some U.S. Indian tribes received some reparations

of some kind from the U.S. government? People fought against our segregation,

Jim Crow laws, and everything else through demonstrations in which a lot of

people died just for African Americans to get the right to vote, to have desegregated

bathrooms and water fountains, to be equal with their white peers, to eat anywhere and at any eating establishment they want. An African American lady refusing

to sit at the back of the bus because she was told to start all those struggles which

gave us our current Civil Rights Laws signed by Lindon Banes Johnson. Looks like

on the reparations issue, the African American descendants of slaves were not even

allowed to sit at the back of the bus but thrown under the bus. How do we fix this? Stay tuned.

Chapter Nine: Individual?

Well this is going to be a one-page chapter. I remember that an African American lady is

running a website where she has a clearing house for white people to donate goods to African

American families or other families in need. Some state colleges have initiated special fees to

pay for descendants of African Americans to get free college. Some billionaires running for

President, such as Michael Bloomberg and Ted Styers, wanted to pay for African Americans

to do so the two could do it together. However, will not (and they are Democrats, go figure). Money spent

on campaign elections could pay for African American reparations 50 times over (media

companies make a ton of money from political candidate's campaigns). It is unlikely that,

though a person's heart or a small group's heart is in the right place, an individual or small group can solve the African American reparations problem nationally. This leads to what

will work? We shall see in later chapters.

Chapter Ten: Bank?

Another short Chapter.   There was talk by African American community about concentrating

all their purchasing power into a bank that is only for African Americans and services African

Americans only. As I understand by our laws this is illegal because it discriminates (in this case

reverse discriminates) against people who are not black who may want to invest in these

enterprises. This goes against Civil Rights and Federal and State Banking laws. So, in

our society this cannot happen…you cannot concentrate all financial power into one race…more

of which will be spoken about later.

Man, this is a short chapter. I thought I catch you, the reader, 'a break'. Let us move on.

Chapter Eleven: Church?

I am going to cut to the chase. As my memory serves, after the Civil War, General Sherman

gave the order in late 1865 to confiscate white family properties and 40 acres and a mule to

give to African Americans as payback for living in the former status of slavery. It was

overturned by Andrew Johnson and property that was given to African Americans confiscated

from the white families was returned to the white families. Compounding 'this felony',

Andrew Johnson repaid former slave holders for the emancipation of their slaves.

Callie House after the Civil War establishing a Freeman's Bureau that went to dust over

mail fraud concerns by white investigators in the early 1900's. Government efforts or

citizens persuading government efforts were not working. What would?

'CRASH!!!!', In the late 1960's, James Foreman and the Black Economic Development

98

Council 'crashed' a Sunday service of a prominent Jewish Church to demand the church

to pay reparations to African Americans nationally…he noted Jewish patron's lives were

worth millions and African Americans were only five bucks. Though Foreman made an

impact, the Jewish synagogue and its Denomination paid extraordinarily little of what Forman asked.

Religious places are wonderful places and they do a lot for a lot of people. They even

have apologized for slavery. I think some religious college took the lead of a private college

and charged a tuition fee so African American students there get free education to make up

for past slavery of African American ancestors. On a national scale however, even if the

Pope of the Catholic church has put up any money to deal with African descendants of

African slaves globally, the Catholic Church would go broke. Religious institutions,

as government institutions, are not ready to put up the money to do this. Businesses?

Many groups have sued businesses who owned slaves in that era for restitution but

failed almost everywhere. What about the current business community? Sounds

promising. Let us keep it moving.

Chapter Twelve: Stocks?

Another short chapter. I do not remember too much about this because it is not practical

here. I remember that in Latin America and third world countries, this would be resolution

to Civil Wars…government forced its Corporations to issue free stock to people who

were formerly repressed as part of a settlement of Latin America civil wars. Reparations

groups have tried to get this kind of thing from Corporations here who were around

at that time using slaves to operate their business but most courts through it out on the

basis of the 1st, 5th, and 14th amendments. I thought I would state it here for historical

reference. Moving On.

Chapter Thirteen: Celebrity Bonds?

I remember back when I was at Texas A and M Commerce that David Bowie and a guy

named David Pullman developed the Celebrity Bond. It was called East Texas State University

back then. I was in college studying political science at my dorm watching MTV when it was

at the time, a newscast about David Pullman and David Bowie creating a new method of

financing called the Celebrity Bond in which an entertainer leverages future royalty

of famed own property in return for upfront cash of which the entertainer or artist will

pay back his investors with interest. David Bowie was the forefront of this…why I

do not know it was a long time ago.

 As rich as most celebrities are…they could not with all their wealth pay back African

American descendants of slavery with their resources...they would be hungry and homeless

(some scholars set African American suffering somewhere in the Trillions of dollars.)

Though this is a nice idea we must try something else because we want all people to

financially affluent because it helps the U.S. economy as a whole...moving onward.

Chapter Fourteen: Tax Break, For Reparations?

When I was studying Political Science at Texas A and M Commerce (back then

East Texas State University), I was studying a method of reparations that was what

I thought totally private. Businesses would donate large sums of money to IRS

for African American redistribution for past crimes of slaves. A Graduate Student

wrote this paper at the time from another school. This would be a totally private

endeavor pitched by IRS to do this and this would be voluntary to individuals and

business owners. I could see the goodwill that could help these individuals and

business owners if they did this. "Hey shop with us...we donated to reparations

fund IRS set up, we are a 'woke' business and we are here to take care of you! Shop with us." Would this be enough incentive to get the voluntary businesses to pitch in

to this IRS reparations fund. The graduate student who wrote this was not sure, so

he suggested the IRS would give tax breaks to businesses that participate. This could

work...but if one went by the opinion of the people, I know in my community...nothing would

motivate anyone to pitch into this fund. They would reply, "they can get a job."

They are probably right...but hey that is what we are trying to do with reparations aren't we?

Let us keep moving on and see.

Chapter Fifteen: Gender Tax?

I believe in restitution for women for the crimes that happen to them and the

crap that they must put up with from men. An Australian article I was reading says we should

tax the difference between the excess pay men make over the women, tax the man, and pay the

woman the difference so there will be equal justice in pay between men and women in that

society or nation. I call this the 'scalp tax'. It would 'scalp' the men's pay (per year) which is in

a lot of cases more than the woman and give this difference to the woman to equal women's

pay out to men, thus equal empowerment and equal rights for women. Women who always

wanted to 'scalp' men for all the crap in the world…here is your chance! Before you pull out

the knives however, it is illegal to have a gender tax, race tax, or anything of that sort in the

U.S. because the First, Fifth, and Fourteenth amendments. Sorry, you ladies will have to

put away your knives. Before you ladies cry, there may be an answer to Women's Reparations

yet. Please keep reading.

Chapter Sixteen: U.S. History Brief.

This is my recollection of American History many years ago. It is noticeably short and out

of my poor little memory cells. I am doing this however to prove a hypothesis so bear with me.

United States formed 1776, Independence from Great Britain.

War of 1812: Cemented our independence from Great Britain.

U.S. Constitution ratified 1788 in place 1789 replacing Articles of Confederation.

The Constitution separated government into three co equal bodies, Executive, Judicial,

Legislative each with checks and balances making them co equal Constitutional Republic.

U.S. oldest Constitutional Republic.

1860-1865 U.S. Civil War won by Union forces against Confederate forces, making Federal

Government supreme law of land as well as emancipating slaves bringing to equality to American society.

1917-1918 Fought World War I with allies and won.

1941-1945 Fought World War II and won.

1960's Cultural Revolution, rebelling against Vietnam War and pushing for Civil Rights Legislation. We lost in Vietnam, Civil Rights passed, however.

1970's Equal Rights Amendment up for ratification and wasn't fully ratified until this year

 2020.   Not in effect because ratification passed deadline of when it should have been ratified.

1980's   Conservative Revolution marked by Ronald Reagan.

1990-2020   Clinton president, George W. Bush president. Fought Gulf Wars I and II and won. As of this writing still stuck in war in Afghanistan, America's longest war surpassing Vietnam.

2008-2016 President Barak Obama president, first black president. Current President Donald J. Trump. Investigation and impeachment of Donald J. Trump for Russians helping him get elected but did not prove anything, so he is still President. Stopped War with North Korea and has economy in good shape.

2016-2020: Rise of Me-Too Movement by women that puts the likes of

Harvey Weinstein, Bill Cosby, and other criminal sexual predators in prison that violate women and children and strengthened laws to incarcerate people who violate people and children, people who do this horrible, insane, satanic, evil.

2019-2020 Corona virus came upon the world scene as a pandemic. United States shut down economically now struggling trying to reopen economy. George Floyd kneed down by police suffocating the African American man (George Floyd) and later Atlanta shooting of black man ignited racial tensions in country waking up lawmakers that structured police reforms was necessary so incidents like this would not happen again. President Donald Trump signed executive order to stop choke holds (as of this writing). After Floyd incident protests turned to riots. Corona virus vaccine may be out later in year as of this writing. Election for President; Former Vice President Joe Biden vs President Donald J. Trump and Vice President Mike Pence for 2020 Presidential race.

This is from my poor little memory as of this writing, if anyone wants further investigation of American History, please consult Google or the local library.

Chapter Seventeen: South African History

It has been a long time since I studied world history…but this is what I remember of South African history. 4th Century A.D. Migrants settle what is now South Africa.

1400's: Portuguese explore South Africa

1600's: Dutch East India Company founded Cape Colony at Table Bay.

1700: British forces seize Cape Colony from Dutch. Early 1800's turned back over to Dutch but ceded back to Great Britain. Slavery and wars with black natives were common under British rule. Two Boers Wars in 1800's.

This is where my memory kicks in because I studied Apartheid in college:

1934: Union of South Africa created independent from Britain. Slavery with blacks have long since ended but two separate societies exist with the whites in power.   Whites control most of the land because their ancestors took that land from the native black population. (We now consider that wrong!)

1948: National Party, whites, take power and start a policy of Apartheid in which everyone is registered by race, so the white minority controls their hold over this mostly black nation and the whites own most of the land.

1950: Nelson Mandela and ANC begin civil disobedience and guerilla warfare to fight Apartheid. Through the following decades Nelson Mandela and ANC conduct civil disobedience and guerilla warfare to have civil equality with white government.

After much international pressure and Nelson Mandela jailed, riots and so forth went on until 1994 Nelson Mandela becomes President of South Africa.   Apartheid has been lifted and there is total equality

117

between whites and people of color, the South African land is held by the white population buyback program initiated by ANC Nelson government to buy back land from whites and redistribute it to people of color to even out land ownership in the nation.

Chapter Eighteen: Expropriation Without Compensation

I have been keeping up with news from Tucker Carlson on Fox and other news channels

about how South Africa is moving forward to a policy of Expropriation without Compensation.

This newer generation of South African people of color are looking to gain 80% of land property still held by white families.

President of South

Africa, Cyril Ramaphosa, is trying to please many factions. The ANC and a more radical group

Economic Freedom Fighters want to seize the land of the white families and redistribute to

people of color for farming purposes. Some white families have threatened to shoot people

who try to take, their land, Cyril Ramaphosa to me is trying to keep his country from going into civil war,

by making Expropriation Without Compensation as easy as possible on people. President

Ramaphosa has released many hectares of State Own land to redistribute to people of color

to be farmers. The South African government will have compulsory training to these

individuals of how to farm before they get the land. However more extreme elements

of the ANC and EFF, parties who a mostly people of color, want a more extreme policy

of taking the land that is now being held by the nation's white families who make up

twenty percent of the population or so but hold ownership of 80 plus percent of South

Africa's land. One can see why South Africa's people of color would be seriously

upset with this when all they can do for their families is rent and not be able to own,

I sort of understand how they feel. I am in current litigation with the State of Texas over the five acres my mom and dad owned. I and my parents had our arguments

but I stayed and helped them out because they were my parents and I loved them.

My mother did not sign the lady bird deed which would have given me the property

over the State of Texas because she was mad that I put her in a home so I could find

a lady and get married. I had to put her into a home because of Adult Protective

Services, Texas Police, forced me too, against her will. I am sad over that. I am

seriously saddened that my own native state government, the State of Texas, did

not see or did not want to see how I cared for my mother as they seized my inheritance

to pay my mother's nursing bills. As I said earlier, give to Cesar's what is Cesar's

give to God what is God and move on. That is what I did.

So, since I lost my inheritance to the State of Texas government, I think I have a unique

experience as to what is like to lose land that you felt that is rightfully years to your

government.   I, however moved on with life to find the good things in life and if there

was any forgiveness due I forgave my mother for me leaving high and dry for putting her

in the senior citizen home.   Right now, in South Africa, people of color want to run

off the white families off their land to get back their land that use to belong to their ancestors.

White families are buying guns to protect their land from people of color. One group is

threatening the other if the other starts something…they will blow them away with

guns and weapons.   If blood be spilt, so be it. President Cyril Ramaphosa is stressing, while the Coronavirus 19 is going on, himself to an early grave trying to keep tensions in his nation from blowing up into

a civil war and a racial war.

My advice to South Africa is this, forgive each other and be the mature adults they

are (or should be) and find a more mature way of equitably distributing the contested

land to everyone's satisfaction. Mandela had in place, after the fall of Apartheid,

a buy-back program where the government that was now led by people of color could buy

back the land from the white families and redistribute it to the disadvantaged population.

Now South Africa is moving away from that by amending their constitution to replace

buyback with Expropriation Without Compensation. The mostly people of color who

lead the government want land distribution to them to go faster. I feel their pain this

124

is their native land. White families do not want their land broke up. This generation

of white folk in South Africa had nothing to do with the slavery and Apartheid that

happened by their ancestors in the past.

What do I suggest to South Africa, The United States, Armenia, and Germany about what kind of reparations they should have? Here is my suggestion.

Chapter Nineteen

<u>Perpetual Commercial Reparations</u>? (It is not ready for prime time, my idea of Perpetual Commercial Reparations should at least be discussed with other views concerning racial, gender, and economic equality for all.)

I have worked for a retail chain for 19 years and my pet hobby was trying to merge

reparations concerns to retail and make a program that would have the same effect as

reparations without taxpayer money or any government being involved. My research

and conclusions for this are in the book "A Case For; Women's Reparations: Perpetual

Commercial Reparations" which is Amazon web store if one

wants to get a copy to study my research.

My program is called Perpetual Commercial Reparations. The following is how my program works:

It works as companies sell retail reparations bonds to community to finance $80000 one

time opportunity as leg up to U.S. historically repressed individuals. This one-time opportunity

can be used for anything under the sun if it is legal. (Savings, college, drug or alcohol rehab, medical operation, car, house, start a business, invent a product, create music or

movie, and so on). The catch is you have 4 years to write a book, produce media, blueprint, or

spec, whatever you did with that money, the rights of story or design, or spec goes to corporation

to continue financing this opportunity for Americans over 18. Investors benefit is return on bond

and these retail reparations bonds though not backed by FDIC or government, is overseen by

SEC to make sure investor is not ripped off and if there is problem, the retail outlet financing

reparations will settle with the individual who was wronged, protecting the reputation of the

bond. Applying for the program as well as investing in the bond can be done by phone app.

Who are the clients or who should be first to be in on this program? How does this compare to Expropriation without Compensation? That is a topic to be discussed in the

following final chapters of the book.

Chapter Twenty: Expropriation Without Compensation vs. Perpetual Commercial Reparations.

I remember being scared and upset as I tried to please Adult Protective Services of Texas

wishes and my mother wishes of not going in a home and no one get her money. Adult

Protective Services wanted to put her in a home and threatened to put me in jail if I did not,

my mother would disown me if I did put her in a home. It had to be a state home because

private homes cost so damn high. I and other relatives got her in there because I did so

she disowned me by not signing the paper, Lady Bird Deed, necessary for me to keep the

home, so now the State of Texas will get the property, Affidavit of Heirship that my mother

signed with me, be dammed.

This is Expropriation Without Compensation, government seizure of property or inheritances.

131

This happened when General Sherman gave Special Order number 15 to give property

belonging to white residents of the Confederacy to African Americans and white residents being

kicked-out of said residences to give it to them. Was this right? Those white residents

enslaved African Americans for many centuries, so I guess the white settlers got what

they deserved at the time. As in the beginning paragraph of this chapter, I did not own

any slaves, I did not hurt anyone, I just did what the State of Texas said to do against

my mother's wishes and I paid for it. The State of Texas is taking the property, my inheritance,

to pay for my mother's nursing care to Medicaid.

The sin I committed in all of this as I have stated before in this book. I, let this destroy the strong bond mother and I had…though she still loved me, and I loved her but as she passed

the bond we had together was gone…I am to blame for that, and for the rest of my life, I will fill like spit.

Cyril Ramaphosa, Current President of South Africa, has a major problem. He has a

few white families owning roughly 80% plus of the land and doing everything to keep

it, even threatening to shoot anyone that threatens to take it from them. Then there are

80% plus of the population who are people of color who are renters or tenants serving

their white landlords or employers, one way or another, on the cheapest dime possible. The only

difference since Apartheid is that South Africa's people of color run the government

and they want to see their leaders in that government not buy back, but take the land outright by force with the South African army or they will do it themselves.

Cooler heads are prevailing though, they are passing an amendment to their constitution

that will give the government power to seize land without compensation. This is what is

being kicked around now in discussions and written opinions sent in by population. When

this is done, their National Assembly will probably pass the amendment for Expropriation

Without Compensation, which will let the government take the land by using local deputies,

the tenants of the land will complain to some government commission, but in most cases the

government will probably prevail and seize the land without compensating its owners. The

government will redistribute the lands to the population who are people of color and the land ownership in South Africa will be more even…avoiding a civil and racial war, hopefully!

According to You tube, President Cyril Ramaphosa is not waiting for the Parliament to act.

Under Cyril's control, the state control since he is President, During the State of the Nation

Address in Parliament he will release 700000 hectares of state land for agricultural production

this year along with, along with 44,000 hectares to settle land restitution claims.

There is a catch to this though, the people of color that are receiving the land must be

undergo compulsory farm training taught by the Government before they get the land. I

am sure that the President wants these people to be farmers and produce for the economy,

not flip the state given property so they can booze and party, party, party. I am sure

President Cyril Ramaphosa will have some contract with the beneficiaries of the state

given land before he releases it to them.

I have cost controls in my Perpetual Commercial Reparations plan when my client

gets the $80000 for whatever purpose they state in their application. They must stick

with what they said the purpose of that $80000 is for, if they go to Vegas or gamble

it away, blow it at a stripper's club, or make purchases that it was not meant for, the

repaid client will go to prison for fraud and owe that sponsoring corporation that

gave them a break $80000.   A second cost control measure is that it is $80000

one time for the lifespan of that individual. There are no second chances. Finally

the retail reparations bond is self-policing, the SEC will catch the corporation's employees that messes with the bond for personal gain and put them in prison, the corporation

that is sponsoring the retail reparations bond will pay back the victim investor. An app on

the people's phone is the portal to the program, either people investing in it, or people applying

for the program. The SEC and law enforcement (government) polices the retail reparations bond

program does not provide financing. The sponsoring corporation of the retail reparations bond is the

one that is putting up the money and risk. The ***opportunity*** is the reparations, people who 'jack' the opportunity will owe the $80000 and go to jail.

According to his State of the Nation address I seen on You tube one night, President Cyril

Ramaphosa is prioritizing South Africa's youth, women, people with disabilities, and those who

have been farming on communal land and are ready to expand their operations for training and allocation of the state given land. To whom will the blessings of my program be distributed?

The next chapter will answer that question.

Chapter Twenty-One: Which System is

Better and Who Should Be Paid?

Of course, I am going to say that my Perpetual Commercial Reparations plan is the best

model there is of all the models mentioned in this book. The government only polices the

program and does not put up any money. A private retail entity puts up the money and

does the reparations in order to gain customers and make more money. Investors make

money in program as well, and historically disadvantaged people are paid back with an

opportunity for all the wrongs done to them or their ancestors in the past.

President Cyril Ramaphosa outlined his historically disadvantaged people in the last paragraph of the last chapter. That was South Africa, what about my program

for the United States and beyond?

I say that women should share in the blessings of my reparation program first. Women

should come first because they are often victims of brutal crimes and they must put

up a lot from men to work and go about their day to survive. Here is my suggested

distribution of the $80,000 perpetual commercial reparations benefit:

1. **Women** of all races, backgrounds, or orientations or economics because of sexual misconduct, sex crimes, human trafficking and discrimination.
2. **African American men** because of slavery and discrimination.
3. **Hispanic American men** because of discrimination and loss of land.
4. **Native American men** because of loss of land and discrimination.
5. **Asiatic American men** (Persian, Russian, Asian, Indian, Chinese, Japanese, and so on from Asia area.)
6. **Muslim American men** (because of discrimination).
7. **White American men** (no longer responsible for slavery).

All humans in U.S. that turn 18 and become an adult would qualify to invest in retail

reparations bond or be able to apply for the $80,000 one-time opportunity if they follow

the rules.

I chose women first not only because of all the criminal sex crimes, sexual misconduct,

sexual harassment, and discrimination. When a ship sinks it is tradition to unload the women

and children first, then the men if you can. If there is no more room, the remaining men

sink with the ship. Well I am not talking about a sinking ship here, but that method has

helped with the distribution of my perpetual commercial reparations model so that is

what I chose to use.

This Perpetual Commercial Reparations model is an original idea I came up with from

the research I have done for "A Case For; Women's Reparations" which is published on Amazon

and Walmart/Kobo e books. The Perpetual Commercial Reparations idea is my idea and the

the ideas I express in my book is mine and mine alone. I am sure there are holes in my model

of reparations and I am willing to claim them. I however am the only person in the U.S. that

can offer a reparations model without use of taxpayer's money, however flawed it may be at

the moment. As people read and discuss my Perpetual Commercial Reparations model maybe

I and fellow Americans can close those holes together.

Recommendations:

Though there was love between my mother and I as she passed, because I betrayed her to obey the State and stay out of jail by doing what I was told and put her in a home, I lost her trust, I was disrespectful and unpatriotic to her because she was the widow of a war veteran who was my father. Loosing that trust, I lost the bond between mother and I had, and I will never get back. I realize as I communicate with God, that God was right, I should lose my inheritance to the State of Texas as the State commanded and has taken. I didn't respect her feelings that she wanted to stay out of the home and keep her freedom because of my greed to inherit the property and sell it so I could marry a beautiful woman and start a family of my own, which unfortunately, has never came to pass. Amen!!!!!!!!!!!!!!!!!!

  Admitting that; I want to make the following recommendations to the following leaders and countries of this world, so they do not make my mistake with their people, thereby causing social calamity and chaos:

a. **Cyril Ramaphosa:** Mr. President of South African, please consider using my Perpetual Commercial Reparations plan along with Nelson Mandela's idea of buying back property from white families and redistribute it to the people of color in your population appropriately to equalize more the ownership of land in your country rather than the Expropriation Without Compensation you are on, otherwise your nation's trust, the bond that holds your economy together, may go away and your economy goes into freefall and your country could wind up in a civil and racial war. Don't lose your bond with your people as I have with my mom because others want you to "Charge In Where Angels Fear to Tread", Burning away the bonds with your people will catch fire, causing South Africa to vaporize to ashes. Keep all the colors of your people together with love and respect for each other.

b. **Turkey:** Make peace with Armenia and U.S. with my program to solve Armenian population or descendant's reparations issues.

c. **United States:** Use my reparations program for national reparations program to uplift our reparations issues uplifting our people in order to honor George Floyd's passing by creating a more peaceful and prosperous society for our American family.

Epilogue:

Thanks to my readers for reading my book of my idea and presentation of Perpetual

Commercial Reparations to solve the reparations problem in the United States. I know

it does not cure the Corona virus that is spreading and causing world chaos presently, I hope

you come away from reading this having something to think on and care about.

Do not Make My Mistake, Be Good To, Your Mothers and Fathers, No Matter What.

Thanks, The Author, Bryan Ray Cook.

Chapter Twenty-Two

Quiz

I have developed a quiz to help you remember key points of this book and American, South African, and World History concerning reparations. This can be done orally, use a piece of paper, or if you have the paperback version of this book, fill in the blanks and circle or match answers with your pen or pencil.   I hope you find this quiz useful. Thanks. Bryan Ray Cook. This quiz also contains common decency questions.

Reparations and Respect:

1. Good morals state one should always care about parents. (Circle True or False)?
2. What are the twelve ways scholars state that reparations could happen?

1._Payout_____

2._Pension_____

3._ Bonds_____

4.__Baby_____

5.__Land_____

6.__Courts_____

147

7. Individual_____

8. Bank_____

9. Church_____

10. Stocks_____

11. Taxbreaks_____

12. Gender Tax_____

American and World History,

3. Are there groups in the world who were paid back for past injustices and violence? Please, fill in blanks of who they are. _Jewish People (Paid By, WWII Germany), World War I Allies (paid by WW1 Germany), Japanese Americans (Paid by United States), Native Americans paid by (United States).

4. When was the Declaration of Independence passed? July 4, 1776.

5. What year was our current U.S. Constitution ratified? Sept. 17, 1787.

6. When year was our U.S. Constitution implemented with bill of rights? _Dec 15, 1791

7. What are the three branches of government in the U.S.? Executive, Judicial, Legislative

8. Who was our first President? George Washington.

9. When was our Civil War? April 12, 1861 – April 9, 1865.

10. What was the one big issue that the North and the South fought over? Slavery of African Americans.

11. Who was President during Civil War? <u>Abraham Lincoln</u>.
12. Who is the President of the United States now? <u>Donald J. Trump.</u>
13. What mostly white European countries took land away from African tribes in what is over a period of centuries is now South Africa? <u>Portugal</u>, <u>Denmark</u>, <u>Great Brittan (U.K)</u>.
14. What South Africa racial practice ended in the 1990's when Mandela was elected? <u>Apartheid.</u>
15. What is the practice of South Africa's land reform idea of Expropriation without Compensation? <u>Take land away from mostly but not necessarily all white families and give it to South African people of color families so they can be farmers.</u>

Common decency questions:

16. Women throughout history have been victims of abuse and sexual assault by men as well as other people. This is the proper behavior that men and other people should have toward women as well as cat calling and lude comments. True or <u>False</u>.

17. George Floyd, who was black, died after being kneed by a white police officer as he was being arrested supposedly for passing a fake twenty-dollar bill. This is the proper behavior of a police officer. True or <u>False.</u>

18. All police officers are bad. True or <u>False.</u>

19. All African Americans are bad. True or <u>False.</u>

20. The whole human race and all the races of it are evil. True or <u>False</u>.

Personal Viewpoint

21. Joe Biden is better than Donald Trump for President (U.S.). Why?

(Various Answers)

_____
_____
_____
_____
_____
_____
_____

22. Donald Trump is better than Joe Biden for President (U.S.) Why?

_____
_____
_____
_____
_____
_____
_____
_____
_____
_____

23. Vice Presidential Candidate Kamala Harris will bring out the African American vote for Joe Biden. Why? (Various Answers)._____

_____
_____
_____
_____
_____
_____
_____
_____

24. The African American vote in the United States is set in stone for the Democratic Party. Why? (Various Answers)

_____

_____

_____

_____

_____

_____

_____

_____

_____

_____

_____

_____

_____

_____

_____

_____

25. After a bitter election between the Biden-Harris ticket and the Trump- Pence Ticket, Joe Biden and Kamala Harris becomes President and Vice President of the United States. Biden and Harris's victory came to be because the African American community carried the day for Biden and Harris. The Democratic Party takes over the Congress. The Democrats realized it is the African American community that brought them to power. The Democrats in Congress and the President now will make sure that African American's are compensated for America's past sin of slavery from the U.S. Treasury, (Federal Government). Will this happen?

_____

_____

_____

_____

_____

_____

_____

_____

_____

_____

_____

_____

_____

_____

_____

_____

_____

The End